U.S. Airborne
Forces
Europe
1942-45
by Brian L. Davis

Published by
Arms and Armour Press
Lionel Leventhal Limited
2-6 Hampstead High Street
London NW3 1PR

SBN 85368 106 6

Series Editor: Brian L. Davis, for
Key Military Publications
Series Design: David Gibbons, for
Arms and Armour Press
Camerawork: Duotech Graphics
Limited

Acknowledgments
The author wishes to acknowledge
the invaluable assistance given by
the following in the preparation of
this book: Dr. Gwyn Baylis and
David Nash of the Imperial War
Museum, London; the Museum of
the Parachute Regiment and
Airborne Forces, Aldershot;
Emmanual Scoulas of Chicago; Roy
Smith; and Alan Beadle. Photographs reproduced are US Official,
by courtesy of the Imperial War
Museum, and from the collection
of the US Army Signal Corps,
Washington (plates 3, 4, 5, 6, 7, 8,
9, 10, 30 and 37).

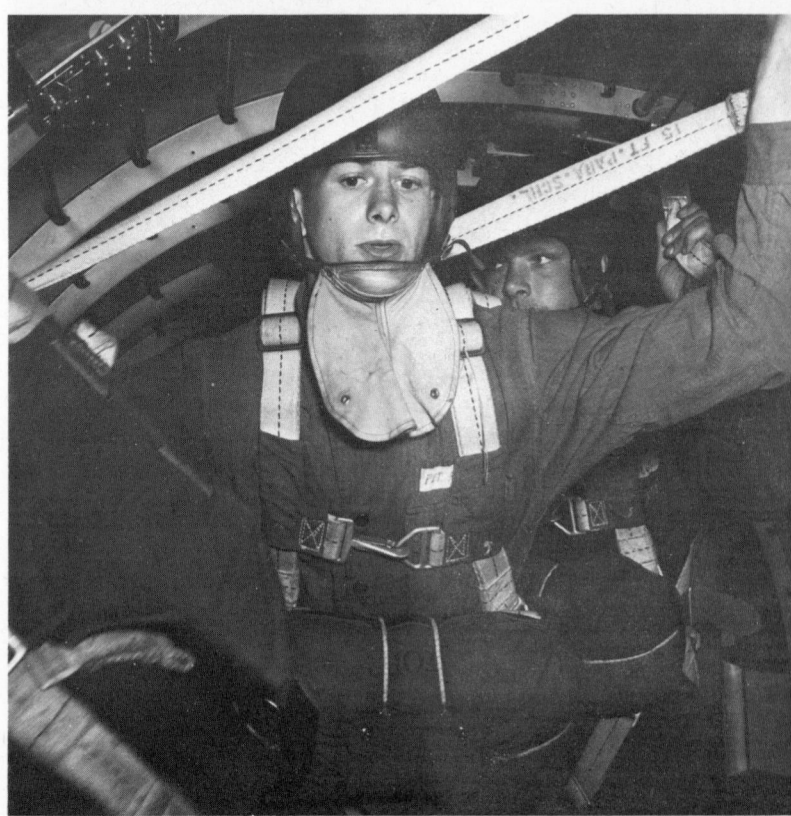

Printed in England

Contents

1. Top: *American C-46s and C-47s with their gliders, lined up on a runway in preparation for the crossing of the Rhine by the 1st Allied Airborne Army.*
2 and 3. *Contrasts in training and combat clothing for paratroopers.*

2. *The command 'go' has been given and the men from the 504th Parachute Infantry Regiment move swiftly to the aircraft's open door.*
3. *The 'jump-off' position, demonstrated here by paratrooper Paul Mahler.*

4 and 5. *Paratroopers at Fort Benning. It is noticeable that a variety of head-dress was used for training purposes during these initial days of the American parachute arm. The early pattern of parachute jump suit can clearly be seen in plate 4.*

Historical Background

American interest in airborne forces was initiated during the First World War. At that time General Mitchell - pioneer of aerial bombardment - originated a project to establish airborne divisions of troops who, in his own words, would "climb over" the impassable Western Front. For various reasons his plan was postponed until the 1919 campaign, and with the coming of the armistice and the end of the war it was dropped altogether.

When the United States entered the Second World War it possessed no military airborne troops: but in 1942 it was well aware of the success of German airborne forces and set about organising its own airborne divisions. The initial training of paratroop instructors was carried out with the co-operation of American fire-fighting personnel who had been trained to parachute into remote wooded areas to combat forest fires.

The activation of the 82nd and 101st US Airborne Divisions
Originally a First World War unit, the 82nd Infantry Division - known as the 'All American' because men from every state in the Union served in its ranks - was reactivated at Camp Clairborne, Louisiana, in March 1942.

On 16th August of the same year the newly formed infantry division was split to form the first American airborne divisions: the 82nd 'All American' Airborne Division and the 101st 'Screaming Eagles' Airborne Division. The 82nd Airborne was immediately moved to Fort Bragg, North Carolina. There it absorbed into its ranks the American 504th Airborne Infantry Regiment, which had come into being at Fort Benning, Georgia, on 1st May 1942. (See plate 3.) Thus the first American parachute regiment became part of one of the first American parachute divisions. (See plates 4, 5.)

The 82nd Airborne Division in North Africa.
Under the command of General Matthew B. Ridgeway, the 82nd was transferred to North Africa. It landed at Casablanca on 10th May 1943 and was moved shortly afterwards first, by rail, to Oujda in Algeria and later, by truck, to Kairouan, Tunisia - the departure point for the division in its airborne invasion of Sicily. (See plate 6.)

The invasion of Sicily and the role played by the 82nd Airborne.
The Allied forces made available for 'Operation Husky', the assault on the island of Sicily, were the US 45th Infantry Division, transferred from the States; the US 3rd Infantry Division, held back from the Tunisian battle in readiness; and the US 1st Infantry Division released from the Tunisian battle-area.

These three divisions were reinforced by the US 2nd Armoured Division, which had been operating in Morocco; paratroop elements of the US 82nd Airborne Division; US Rangers, who were to spearhead the attack; a Canadian corps sent from the United Kingdom; and the British Eighth Army, part of the strength of which was detached before the end of the Tunisian campaign to prepare for the assault.

On the night of 9th/10th July 1943 paratroop elements from the 82nd Airborne Division, comprising the 505th Parachute Regiment and the 3rd Battalion of the 504th Parachute under the command of Colonel James 'Jumping Jim' M. Gavin, took off from their base at Kairouan in North Africa. Their task was to parachute into Sicily to spearhead the Allied seaborne invasion of the island. But before they could reach their dropping zone, tragedy overtook the 'All Americans'. As their

6. *A soldier of the 505th Parachute Infantry Regiment photographed at Oujda, North Africa, 30th June 1943.*

5

planes approached the island, they were mistaken for the Luftwaffe by the gunners on the American naval vessels taking part in the seaborne invasion. Many of the C-47s were destroyed by these marksmen, whose accuracy was so unfortunate on this occasion. Despite the great loss in men and equipment, however, the survivors landed as planned and carried out their allotted tasks to the full. (See plates 7, 8.) Ten days after the initial landings, the regiments were withdrawn to their base.

It was the opinion of General der Flieger Kurt Student - Chief of Staff of all German parachute forces from 1943-5 - that the Allied airborne operation in Sicily was decisive in spite of the widely scattered air-drop, unavoidable in a night landing. According to him, it was the blocking action of the 82nd Airborne Division that prevented the Panzer Division Hermann Göring from reaching the beachhead, thus denying the Germans the opportunity of driving the Allied seaborne forces back into the sea. At his trial at Nuremberg, General Student stated: "I attribute the entire success of the Allied Sicilian operation to the delaying of German reserves until sufficient forces had been landed by sea to resist the counterattacks by our defending forces."

The 82nd Airborne Division in Italy

The 82nd Airborne flew back to Sicily from North Africa to prepare for the Allied invasion of Italy, in which it was earmarked to support the landings. It was to jump 40 miles north of Salerno and 20 miles north of Naples, along the Volturno river, to destroy the bridges from Capua to the sea and impede German troops attempting to reinforce the defenders of Salerno. But the mission was cancelled at the last moment. With the Italian surrender and the fear that the Germans would occupy Rome and take prisoner the Italian royal family and government, the airborne troops were switched instead to preparations for a jump on the Italian capital. Again at the last moment - indeed, three minutes before the scheduled take-off - the jump on Rome was called off. By then, it was too late to employ the 'All Americans' in Operation Avalanche and they were stood down.

When the Allied landings at Salerno became a shambles, the 82nd were called on to make a drop at very short notice in support of the ground troops. With the tragic Sicilian episode of two months before still fresh in their minds, two battalions of paratroopers boarded their C-47s; and shortly before midnight on 13th September 1943 they jumped on to the Salerno beachhead near Paestum, from where they were rapidly moved by lorry to the defensive positions around the beachhead. (See plate 9.) The whole of the 82nd Airborne was eventually committed to the breakout from Salerno and the move on Naples. And when Naples had been occupied by units of Lieutenant-General McCreery's (British) 10 Corps they were sent to police the city.

The 504th Parachute Infantry Regiment - part of the 82nd Airborne Division - had served at Anzio, and the Italian campaign was climaxed for them when their 3rd Battalion received the Presidential Unit Citation from Major-General Mark Clark, for their part in the Anzio fighting, at a ceremony held at Bagnoli.

With Naples secure, the 82nd were withdrawn from Italy by ship to the United Kingdom, where they arrived at Liverpool on 22nd April 1944 to prepare for their next mission - the D-Day landings.

7 and 8. *Men of the 82nd Airborne*

Division in Italy.

The 101st Airborne Division, from training to D-Day.

A few weeks after its activation on 16th August 1942, the 101st Airborne Division - under the command of Major-General William Carey Lee (plate 10), assisted by Brigadier-General Don F. Pratt - followed the 82nd to Fort Bragg, North Carolina, where it underwent its initial parachute training. (See plate 11.) In the spring of 1943 that training was put to the test during a ten-day manouvre in South Carolina; and in June 1943 the division moved to Tennessee for the Second Army war games. Here the glidermen and parachutists trained with full equipment, practised mass jumps and glider flights and marched hundreds of weary miles up and down the Tennessee hillsides.

A year after their introduction the Screaming Eagles, toughened by the war games, had become a formidable fighting force. And in August 1943 the division began preparations for movement overseas.

Shortly afterwards the 101st left Camp Shanks, N.Y., sailed from New York to Liverpool and then travelled by train to Newbury, where it had its base and headquarters while in the United Kingdom. Manouvres were carried out in the West Country.

As part of their training programme in connection with the proposed invasion of Europe, the men of the 101st learned British communications procedures, examined British equipment and familiarised themselves with details of German military uniforms and equipment, studying charts, photographs and documents. And jump and glider training programmes were undertaken as dress rehearsals for the forthcoming invasion. (See plates 12, 13, 14.) Infantry, engineers, artillery, ordnance, supply, air crews and commanders worked in close co-operation during the weeks before the Normandy landings, polishing details of the team-work that would be vital to the success of the mission. Staff officers carefully checked and scrutinised their maps, charts, aerial reconnaissance photographs and orders; pilots flew practice formations; and the parachutists and glidermen of the 101st put the final polish to the loading and jumping techniques to be employed in the airborne thrust.

The assault on Normandy: D-Day, 6th June 1944

The assault on the French mainland was planned to begin with the dropping of three airborne divisions behind the Atlantic Wall during the night of 5th/6th June, immediately prior to the main seaborne invasion. These divisions - the British 6th Airborne in the Orne Valley and the US 82nd and 101st Airborne at the base of the Cotentin peninsula - were to secure the flanks of the Allied bridgehead and weaken the German beach defences at key-points by attacks from the rear.

The 101st on D-Day

Shortly before D-Day the command of the 101st was relinquished by General Lee, because of ill health, and his place was taken by his assistant General Pratt. For about a week before the invasion started, the men of the 101st sat expectantly in half a dozen marshalling points scattered throughout England. During their working days they tried on and adjusted their parachutes (plate 15), packed the Parapaks and secured them to the bellies of the swarms of C-47s that covered the airfields (plate 16,) loaded and carefully lashed equipment into the fragile CG4a gliders and the sturdier Horsas, and drew their ammunition, grenades, rifle bandoliers, carbine and Tommy-gun clips, machine-gun boxes and belts, and bazooka and mortar rounds.

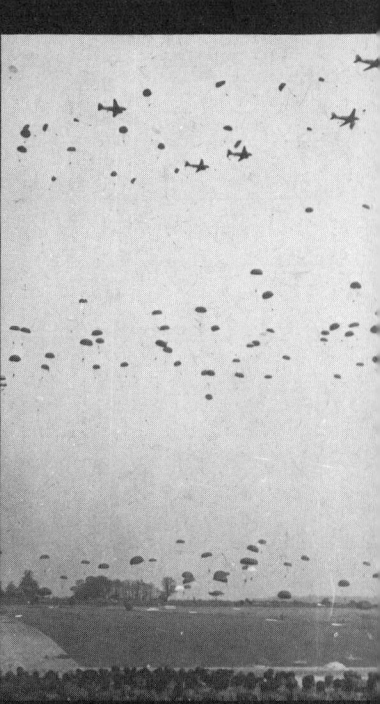

11

15

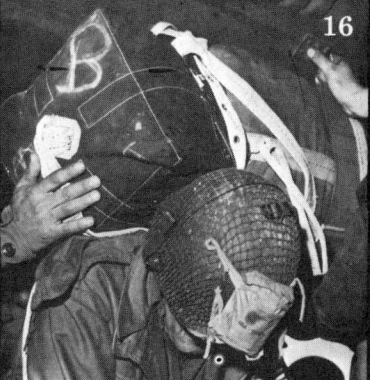

16

9. *Lieutenant-General Mark W. Clark, Commanding Officer, 5th US Army, congratulating men from the 82nd Airborne on their success in the Salerno sector, Italy, September 1943.*

10. *Lieutenant-Colonel William C. Lee, commander of the parachute group at Fort Benning. Lee was later to command the 101st Airborne Division as a major-general.*

11. *Paratroop recruits undergoing training.*

12. *Paratroopers help each other to harness up before entering their Douglas troop-carrying planes for a training exercise in England.*

13. *The jump-masters pacing the jump off.*

14. *A mass airborne exercise.*

15. *A final check is made of equipment preparatory to the landings in Normandy.*

16. *A parapack is shouldered into position to be slung below the belly of the troop-carrying aircraft.*

Demolitionists, radiomen, mortar and machine-gun squads of the parachute regiments tested the heavy loads with which they would jump. In well-guarded quarters the men were briefed by their officers, using maps and models, on terrain, weather, objectives and expected resistance. (See plate 17.) Transport pilots, glider pilots and crews studied their part of the aerial teamwork that would be required to bring a long sky train, under an umbrella of fighters, over the drop zones of Normandy. Supreme Commander Dwight Eisenhower visited the Screaming Eages, or Eaglemen, in their marshalling areas on 5th June. (See plate 18.) It would be on the success of the sky-soldiers' mission that the overall success of the invasion depended.

On the evening of June 5th the glidermen of the 101st stepped into their flimsy craft, and the parachutists boarded their C-47s. (See plate 19.) The 101st Airborne Division had been assigned missions involving the capture of causeways leading from the invasion beaches and the destruction of bridges across roads vital to German communications.

When the lead echelons of Allied aircraft reached the French coast, a thick barrage of anti-aircraft fire enveloped them. Some gliders, forced to cut loose from damaged tow planes, crash-landed in the Channel; and many of the transport planes met a similar fate. But the large majority of the sky armada flew inland in the early morning darkness of 6th June.

Thousands of parachutists spilled from their rocking tracer-scored transports, and gliders circled down from the flak-filled sky. The flak was so dense that jump formations were broken and sticks of paratroopers were scattered over an area fifteen miles wide by twenty-five miles long, some troops dropping even further afield. The widely dispersed jump and glider landings, aided by irregular but stiff enemy resistance encountered almost immediately, prevented the men from forming fully assembled units. Instead, the division - reduced to isolated bands of mixed personnel of a total effective strength of less than a single regiment - fought their way towards their divisional objectives.

A wide area of the Cotentin peninsula was dotted with groups of roving artillerymen, clerks, infantrymen, engineers and cooks engaging the enemy at countless points. The division had lost a great quantity of equipment and almost its entire gliderborne artillery, much of it in the floods of the Merderet and Douve rivers. But the paratroopers had been so well briefed that the situation in which they found themselves and the lack of equipment merely hampered them without halting them. Trained to be individual fighters, and schooled in the use of whatever weapons were available, the odd assortment of servicemen that roamed the hedgelined Normandy fields defeated a panicked enemy at almost every turn. (See plate 20.)

By dawn on D-Day the 101st had mustered 1,100 men out of its original 6,600; and by evening of the first day this number had grown to 2,500. So great was the confusion created in the enemy by the scattering of the American paratroopers in their midst that the reserve forces needed to support the German beach defences could not get through.

General Pratt, who had succeeded to the command of the division just before the commencement of the invasion, was killed in action on the first day of the landings. His glider crashed as he led the 101st glider forces into Normandy, and his place was taken by Major-General Maxwell Taylor.

It was over the swampy approaches to Carentan (plate 21), subsequently captured by the 101st, that Lieutenant-Colonel Cole, battalion commander of the 502 Parachute Infantry, led

17. **Above:** *With the aid of a sand table, Lieutenant-Colonel Edson D. Raff (right) goes over operational details with his assistant, Major Doyle.*
18. **Below left:** *"We will accept nothing less than full victory." General Dwight D. Eisenhower, Commander-in-Chief of the Allied Expeditionary Force, addressing men of the 101st Airborne Division.*

his men in a ferocious bayonet charge - said to have been the first American bayonet charge of the war in Europe. For his gallantry in the action, Colonel Cole - who was later killed in Holland - was awarded the Medal of Honour. And for their part in the costly capture of Carentan, most of the units of the division were awarded the Presidential Unit Citation.

The 82nd on D-Day

The task of the 82nd Airborne Division was to drop astride the Merderet river, south and west of the town of Ste.Mère-Église, extend the flank protection westward by destroying two more bridges over the river Douve and secure the Merderet crossings, thus blocking any attempt by the Germans to contain the Allied invasion forces behind the inundations and opening the way for an early drive to the west coast of the Cotentin peninsula.

The story of the 82nd Airborne Division during the D-Day landings was similar to that of the 101st, except that the 82nd had more success. Its troop-carriers and gliders had to fly a steady course at 1,000 feet in moonlight over an area that was thick with 88mm flak-guns and searchlights, heavily garrisoned, and unsuitable for large-scale landings from the air. The country-side had been deliberately flooded and obstructions had been set up in the only open areas. Because of its close-set and heavy hedgerows, the remainder of the countryside was ideal for defence but extremely difficult to assault.

Allied night-fighters had attempted to sweep the way clear and heavy cloud covered the approach of the airborne Path-finders shortly after midnight on June 6th, so they and the first flight of troop-carriers managed to get through without serious difficulty. But later formations lost cohesion in the clouds and many aircraft drifted off their course. By the time they were clear of the cloudbank, they were already approaching the dropping-zones and it was too late for those that had gone astray to search for the Pathfinder beacons - some of which had been set up in the wrong places. Only 38 out of 120 Pathfinders dropped directly on to their targets. The rest dropped miles away. Flak became more intense and the pilots took avoiding action. Consequently, when the paratroopers were due to leap, 'many planes were flying at excessive speeds and at altitudes higher than those ideal for jumping' (After-Action Report, 82nd Airborne Division, June 1944).

19. Below right: *Paratroopers boarding their C-47s, 5th June 1944.*

Fortunately for the Americans, the anti-aircraft fire was generally ineffective. The German guns, not being laid by radar, succeeded in shooting down only 20 of the 805 American troop carriers that were over the Cotentin peninsula that night. But the aircraft were spared mainly by the bad weather and the wild manoeuvres of the pilots - which paradoxically combined to gravely prejudice the success of the mission.

The 82nd, commanded by Major-General M.B. Ridgeway, was in luck. Its leading regiment - commanded by Lieutenant-Colonel Krause - had the advantage of surprise, and three-quarters of the men landed within three miles of the dropping zone on both sides of the Merderet river. They rallied quickly. By 0400 hours - two hours after the main drop and four hours before the beach force landings - they had taken Ste.Mère-Église, thus establishing a solid base and blocking the Cherbourg-Carentan road. (See plate 22.) But then their real difficulties had set in: only 22 of the 52 gliders carrying guns, transport and signals equipment managed to find the landing zone. The enemy forestalled their attempt to seize the bridges over the Merderet, and the division was therefore split by an almost impassable belt of river and swamp.

West of the Merderet only four per cent of the 82nd's other two regiments were dropped accurately, many of the remaining troops drowning in the flooded countryside under the weight of their weapons and equipment. Survivors were scattered over the eastern half of the area, which was garrisoned by the German 91st Infantry Division - a formation that had been specially trained to combat air-landing operations. By a stroke of good fortune, a party of American paratroopers succeeded in ambushing and killing the German divisional commander, who was returning to his headquarters from an 'exercise conference'. The Americans were so widely scattered and so heavily engaged in fighting for their survival in isolated pockets, however, that they could not proceed to the execution of their principle tasks - the blowing of the Douve bridges and the establishment of a compact bridgehead west of the Merderet to protect the crossings. Almost a third of each regiment had come down east of the river; but the remainder, fighting indomitably in small parties, prevented the 91st Infantry Division from counter-attacking the landings.

In the pre-dawn darkness of D-Day the Germans counter-attacked across the Merderet in strength and were stopped short only 400 yards from General Ridgway's command post; and soon after dawn the remaining German reserves in the Cotentin peninsula were ordered into action. The brunt of their attack fell on the 82nd Airborne Division, upon whom the Americans had reported earlier: 'short 60% infantry, 90% artillery, combat efficiency excellent' (After-Action Report, 82nd Airborne Division, June 1944).

Dawn had found the Americans hard-pressed and short of ammunition, but soon after 0700 hours reinforcements came in by glider and supplies were dropped by parachute. At 1000 hours there was direct contact with the seaborne forces, by which time the glider-infantry were in position along the Merderet river. Against that line the Germans attacked in vain. This successful defence and a two-mile advance north-west by the US 4th Infantry Division gave the American VII Army Corps a bridgehead eight miles deep and nine miles wide by nightfall on D-Day+1.

In the thirty-three days of ferocious fighting before they were finally evacuated back to the United Kingdom, the 82nd Airborne suffered 40% casualties. During that time they successfully engaged five enemy divisions - the 77th, 91st, 243rd, 265th and the 353rd - virtually putting an end to the 91st and 265th as effective fighting units. They also destroyed 62 German tanks and knocked out 44 anti-tank guns and artillery pieces. (See plate 23.)

Of the men of the 101st and the 82nd who had flown across the Channel over a month before, little more than half returned in early July. The rest had been evacuated earlier to hospitals in England - or had been buried in graves in France: for the success of the mission had been acomplished only with great loss of life. (See plate 24.)

The Arnhem operation

During their period of rest and training in the United Kingdom, the depleted ranks of the 82nd and 101st were brought up to strength in readiness for the coming Arnhem operation. (See plates 25, 26.)

Three airborne divisions were to be dropped in column from north to south along the line Arnhem-Nijmegen-Eindhoven. Their task would be to seize the road bridges over the rivers Maas, Waal and Neder Rijn, as well as over five other waterways,

20. *The threat of cold steel. An American paratrooper holds a German soldier prisoner at the point of his bayonet. A somewhat posed photograph taken during the American advance through Normandy.*

21. *Paratroopers of the 101st Airborne Division clear enemy snipers from the wrecked buildings of Carentan.*

22. *The bodies of American troops lying among the wreckage of a Horsa glider that crashed into a wall outside Ste. Mère Église during the initial airborne landings on the night of 6th June 1944.*

23. *In an area under German mortar fire, Lieutenant-General Omar N. Bradley, Commanding General of the 1st US Army in France, decorating officers and men of the 82nd 'All American' Airborne Division.*

24. *Their faces covered by a parachute, eight members of an American airborne unit, killed while landing in Normandy, laid out beside the wreckage of their gliders awaiting burial.*

25. *On their return from Normandy, troops of the 82nd Airborne Division are reviewed by General Eisenhower at a parade held in the United Kingdom on 10th August 1944. The officers on the saluting base are, from left to right: Major-General James M. Gavin, Commanding General of the 82nd Airborne Division; General of the Army Dwight D. Eisenhower, Supreme Commander-in-Chief Allied Expeditionary Force; Major-General Mathew B. Ridgeway, Commanding General of the XVIII Airborne Corps; and Lieutenant-General Lewis H. Brereton, Commanding General of the 1st Allied Airborne Army.*

20 21

22 23

24 25

thus clearing a corridor for the British armoured and motorised columns that would be driving north from the Meuse-Escaut Canal to the Zuider Zee. General Montgomery's intention was to cut Holland in two with this one thrust. establishing the Second Army beyond the Rhine on the plains of northern Germany without having to cross the Rhine and the Maas and outflanking the Siegfried Line defences, which ended in the area of the Reichswald. If all went well, the armour should reach the Zuider Zee on the fourth or fifth day.

Because the airborne forces were to form a corridor fifty miles long, the three divisions had to be landed in depth. The British 1st Airborne Division. commanded by Major-General R. E. Urquhart, supported by the Polish Parachute Brigade, commanded by General Sosabowski, was to drop beyond the Neder Rijn, west of Arnhem.* The 82nd Airborne Division commanded by Major-General James Gavin, was to land between the Maas and the Waal, south of Nijmegen; and the 101st Airborne Division, commanded by Major-General Maxwell Taylor, was to drop between Veghel and Zon, north of Eindhoven. The British 1st and the US 82nd airborne divisions were to operate under the command of British Headquarters 1 Airborne Corps, commanded by Lieutenant-General F.A.M.Browning, which was also to land south of Nijmegen. (See plate 27.) A fourth division, the 52nd Lowland, would be available to be brought in by Dakota transport as soon as an airfield had been captured.

Arnhem and the 82nd

Major-General Gavin was to be responsible for attacking and securing four objectives: three bridges - over the Maas at Grave (the longest in Europe), over the Waal at Nijmegen, over the Maas-Waal Canal - and the Groesbeek Ridge, which runs along the German frontier and dominates the area between the Maas and the Waal.

Because these objectives were so widely separated, General Gavin decided to concentrate his initial landings around Grave and along the Groesbeek Ridge. There would be no point in attempting to seize the Nijmegen bridge until all the other missions had been accomplished.

The Allied air fleet of more than a thousand troop carriers and nearly five hundred gliders, protected by 1,240 fighters, flew into Holland during the afternoon of Sunday, 17th September 1944. Preparing the way for the aerial armada was a force of more than a thousand bombers, which blasted enemy anti-aircraft batteries along the route and around the dropping zones. Except for fifteen FW.190s encountered over Wesel, there was no sign of the Luftwaffe.

The Americans in the Nijmegen-Eindhoven stretch of the corridor met less opposition than that encountered by the British. They were also more successful. Of the relatively few Germans to be seen near the dropping zones, most fled.

By dropping astride the Maas bridge at Grave, one battalion from the 82nd gained this vital objective within an hour of landing. And before it was dark, Gavin's troops had secured the route into Nijmegen by capturing one of the bridges over the Maas-Waal Canal and establishing a cordon across the neck of the rivers along the Groesbeek Ridge.

By the afternoon of 18th September the Irish Guards of the Guards Armoured Division had joined forces with the American 101st Airborne at Eindhoven. The way was then clear for the armour to race on through the corridor to Nijmegen just as

* See British Parachute Forces, 1940-45 (Key Uniform Guide 2)

soon as the destroyed bridge at Zon had been rebuilt - a task that was to take the sappers no more than twelve hours to complete.

The second airborne wave, of reinforcements sent out from England to supply the units fighting desperately on the ground, was almost entirely made up of tugs and gliders - slow, unwieldy combinations incapable of taking violent evasive action to protect themselves. Nevertheless, the fighter screen was so effective that of the 1,203 gliders that took off from England only 13 were shot down. It was the weather rather than the Luftwaffe that prevented these reinforcements from arriving on time. In England heavy fog, lying thick on the assembly airfields, delayed the departure of the gliders and transporters. And in Holland, during the morning of 18th September, the airborne troops on the ground anxiously awaited the reinforcements.

The Germans counter-attacked from the Reichswald and overran the landing zones of the 82nd Airborne Division just before the gliders were due to arrive. General Gavin, unaware that his reinforcements had left England two hours late, thought that he had no time left to warn off or redirect the incoming pilots. Expecting the gliders to appear overhead at any minute, the Americans counter-attacked with a desperate fury and succeeded in driving the Germans back with just thirty minutes to spare. Despite this, the gliders landed under fire and it took all the men Gavin could muster to hold off the enemy.

Their late arrival saved the gliderborne troops from heavy casualties, but it destroyed any chance there had been of capturing the Nijmegen bridge that day.

During the night of 19th/20th September, while a battle-group of the 10.SS-Panzer-Grenadier-Division was being ferried across the Neder Rijn to stiffen the Nijmegen garrison, General Horrocks and General Browning made a fresh plan designed to gain full possession of the Nijmegen road bridge by concerted attacks from north and south. On the next day the 504th Parachute Regiment was assigned the task of crossing the river Waal a mile downstream and seizing the northern end of the bridge, coincident with an attack on the German southern defences by the Grenadier Guards and a battalion of paratroopers. First, however, Nijmegen had to be cleared of German forces so that the assault troops could gain access to the south bank of the Waal.

This mopping-up took the whole of the Wednesday morning, and it was nearly 1500 hours before the 504th were in a position to launch their assault boats into the fast-moving river. Only half the boats carrying the first wave of paratroopers managed to reach the north bank. The rest were destroyed by enemy fire or swept away by the strong river current. But some two hundred men, undaunted, scrambled or swam ashore and established a slender foothold that was gradually reinforced and expanded as the afternoon wore on. This bold assault in clear daylight across a heavily defended river that was 400 yards wide was a most brilliant and courageous feat, and it was duly rewarded. By 1830 hours the Americans had routed the enemy opposition and were advancing towards the road bridge. En route they secured the northern end of the railway bridge, and there they raised the Stars and Stripes.

When General Dempsey met General Gavin after this exploit, he said, "I am proud to meet the commander of the greatest division in the world today" - an opinion endorsed by many other British officers who saw the 82nd Airborne Division in action that day.

26. **Above left:** *Troops of the newly-formed 1st Allied Airborne Army, all of whom had seen service in France, march past General Eisenhower during the review of 10th August 1944.*

27. **Below left:** *Major-General 'Jumping Jim' Gavin (right) conferring with Lieutenant-General 'Boy' Browning near Graves, Holland, after British armour had entered the town.*

28. **Below:** *Men of the 82nd Airborne Division — part of the 1st Allied Airborne Army — receive a last-minute briefing at an airfield somewhere in England before taking off for Holland. The wartime censor has obliterated the divisional shoulder sleeve insignia.*

Arnhem and the 101st

In England, the men of the 101st withdrawn from the Normandy fighting were given a brief rest and were then re-equipped and prepared for another mission. Newly-arrived replacements made up the strength and the division moved again to its marshalling areas, tried on parachutes and had all but boarded the aircraft when the rapidly moving armour of General Patton's Third Army overran the objectives for which they had been earmarked. A second stand-to was called and again events overtook the preparations.

The third move to the airfield was no dry run, and on 17th September 1944 the Screaming Eagles took to the sky for drop zones in Holland near the important city of Eindhoven. (See plate 29.) The 101st formed part of the 1st Allied Airborne Army - the largest mass of troops and equipment ever assembled for an airborne operation. So vast was the force that while the lead elements were spilling from their aircraft over Dutch soil the last echelons of the flight were just taking off from fields in England.

Minutes before the vanguard arrived over the dropping zones, the Germans opened up with all their available flak. Many sticks of parachutists leaped from flaming transports that were held steadily on course until all the occupants were out. Formation was maintained, and pilots even lessened speed during the jump in spite of the intense anti-aircraft fire. Not until all of the airborne troops had left their craft did pilots attempt to take evasive action against the heavy ack-ack fire - and in many cases it was then too late, smudges of black smoke marking the place where planes crashed around the drop zones. (See plate 30.) The daring of the pilots was undoubtedly largely responsible for the well-patterned drop and consequent speedy action.

No significant opposition was encountered on the ground, allowing units to assemble quickly and move out to secure their objectives. These were the highway bridges over a road distance of 15 miles, which had to be taken for the British armoured elements driving up from the south.

Landing near Vechel, the 501st Parachute Infantry Regiment was unopposed in its immediate seizure of all its four bridges. The 502nd Parachute Infantry Regiment seized the main highway bridge near St. Oedenrode. The 506th Parachute Infantry Regiment, landing at Zon, seized the canal-crossing - but the enemy had blown the bridge. On D-Day+1, shortly after noon, the 506th took the key city of Eindhoven with all water crossings intact. During those first two days the division encountered only light opposition.

D-Day+3 saw well organised reinforcements of German infantry and armour counter-attacking units of the 101st at several points. Their penetrations were deep, and in some cases German tanks and infantry moved to within 500 yards of vital bridges.

German bombers, unhampered by anti-aircraft fire, leisurely circled Allied supply convoys passing through the large cities and dropped their bombs on them. They also bombed Eindhoven, killing more than two hundred civilians.

Vechel was the scene of great destruction as German artillery rained a continual barrage of shells on the town from all sides. And twice the Germans cut the road - first a few thousand yards above Vechel and then an equal distance below it. Both attacks were successfully repelled by the outnumbered Eaglemen.

Although the seventy-three-day action in Holland was the least publicised of the division's campaigns, the battle of 'Hells Highway' - in which foot-soldiers of the 101st and British tank

29. Top: *Paratroopers of the 101st Airborne Division — part of the 1st Allied Airborne Army dropped over Holland — board their transport plane at an airfield somewhere in England.*

30. *Troops from the 101st Airborne, having landed safely behind the German lines in Holland, examine what is left of one of their gliders that 'cracked-up'. 18th September 1944.*

crews and artillery worked in close co-operation in the protection of the vital Holland corridor - and the vicious and costly battle of Opheusden, situated between Nijmegen and Arnhem, were probably the most savagely fought single actions in the history of the 101st Airborne Division.

Following the long vigilance on the Neder-Rijn river, the action in Holland - aided whenever and wherever possible by the Dutch underground resistance movement - was drawn to its close when the 101st was withdrawn to Camp Mourmelon, France, on 27th November 1944.

The German Ardennes offensive and Bastogne

When the German forces launched their Ardennes offensive in December 1944, Bastogne - a quiet town in the Belgian Ardennes - lay in the general path of advance of the German Fifth Panzer Army, whose orders were to by-pass the town if it was defended. The leading troops were to rush on to the west and then swing north to join in the main advance towards Antwerp and the coast.

The American garrison at Bastogne at this time was a quartermaster bakery - for an anxious period of time the only Allied troops between the German Army and Antwerp

The 101st had just settled in at their muddy base camp at Mourmelon-le-Grand when a frantic alert for Bastogne was issued. The campaign in Holland had left the sky-soldiers sparsely equipped, and it was in a miscellany of uniforms that they boarded trucks a few hours after the alert and headed for the Belgian Ardennes. Officers and men who had just returned from leave pulled fatigue clothes over their dress uniforms, grabbed helmets and rifles and went along. One battalion of paratroopers, on leave in Paris, missed the operation altogether - as did Major-General Maxwell Taylor, who was in Washington when his division was committed and whose place was taken by Brigadier-General Anthony C. MacAuliffe. The majority of the troops that went in were without ammunition throughout the journey, only receiving some as they left the trucks to march to the front. But the rapid transfer of the 11,000-strong Eagle Division from Camp Mourmelon to Bastogne - a distance of 100 miles in well under twenty-four hours - was a remarkable feat of transportation, accomplished so quickly because the convoys travelled by night with lights on as far as the Belgian border.

On 17th December 1944 the XVIII Airborne Corps with its two divisions - the 82nd and the 101st - had been released to General Bradley by the Supreme Commander and directed towards Bastogne. This preparatory move was not in anticipation of the battle that developed in the area but merely because Bastogne, with four highways meeting in its vicinity, was such an excellent road centre. Troops there could later be despatched by the commander on the spot to any region where they were required.

The airborne troops were pushing towards the front on the 18th December when the situation became so serious on the northern front that General Bradley diverted the leading division, the 82nd, towards the left while the 101st continued on its original course to Bastogne. When the Screaming Eagles began closing on the town during the night of 18th December, the roads out of the town were jammed with retreating troops and vehicles. During that night and on the 19th, while the Germans were occupied with isolated detachments of the troops that had manned the original defensive line, the 101st prepared to defend Bastogne. Not knowing if the town was completely surrounded, the Screaming Eagles prepared for all-round defence;

and although the assaulting German Panzer-Lehr Division by-passed Bastogne to participate in the attack to the north-west, the Americans were under constant pressure from other German units from that moment onwards.

Enemy forces, in the ratio of four to one, at first routed divisional units from hastily constructed defences north of Bastogne. Part of the 506th Paratroop Infantry Regiment entered Noville, about 8 kilometres north of the town, and was pounded mercilessly by direct fire from guns dug in on the hills around the town. Swarms of German tanks and infantry repeatedly overran the undermanned positions of the defenders, and the front line wavered dangerously.

A ceaseless barrage of artillery and night bombing reduced Bastogne to rubble. The wounded were sent back from the front only to lie helpless in a town under a continual rain of shellfire. Surrounded, evacuation was impossible. Some doctors and technicians were captured when the division's aid station was overrun, and this put an even greater burden on the already overworked and under-equipped medical men. One hospital suffered a direct hit in a bombing raid and only two patients survived. Confidently, Radio Berlin reported that the 101st Airborne Division had been annihilated .

The defence of Bastogne consisted of continuous counter-attacks on all sides, in which Belgium's cold winter was an added hazard. Trench-foot and frozen limbs accounted for as many casualties as the German artillery and small-arms. The men fashioned crude jackets for themselves from blankets and tarpaulins, and they made scarves from supply parachutes. Even cooks and clerks fought. And when four Germans came forward under a white flag of truce to deliver a surrender demand to the garrison, commander MacAuliffe tersely gave them his now-famous retort - "Nuts!".

On 22nd December supplies were flown in to the beleaguered garrison, men of the Pathfinder group jumping to mark the zones for the supply drops. The siege dragged on; but the tide of the German winter offensive had turned. The wreckage of enemy armour and equipment cluttered the roads and littered the slopes of the countryside as a result of the replenishment of supplies by air to the artillery of the 9th and 10th Armoured Division. A subsequent air mission provided doctors, technicians and medical supplies. Meanwhile, to the south, hard-hitting tanks of the US 4th Armoured Division were smashing their way

On the infrequent days of flying weather the sky over Bastogne swarmed with P-47s, circling and diving to strafe and bomb the concentrations of enemy troops and armour in Foy and Noville and the close-packed German supply convoys strung out along the Bastogne-Houffliaze road. But the front line was so indefinite that the American troops were too often bombed and strafed in error. The Germans had captured numerous American vehicles, the identification panels of which added to the difficulties of the Air Corps in determining where the enemy was situated.

The relief of Bastogne came at 1945 hours on 26th December 1944 when the lead tanks of the crack American Fourth Armoured Division made contact with a road-block manned by men of the 101st on the southern perimeter. For over a week the Eaglemen had been completely cut off by savagely attacking elements of eight German divisions, whose armour had stabbed in vain at the stubbornly held line while artillery of all calibres had pounded the frozen little town into rubble. When the Fourth Armoured broke through on 26th December, accompanying war-correspondents looked at the levelled buildings,

31. Above left: *Major-General Ridgeway.*
32. Above right: *Major-General Gavin, at 37 years of age, was one of the youngest generals in the US Army.*
33. Below: *Major-General Maxwell D. Taylor (left), Commanding General of the 101st Airborne Division, shakes hands with*

Brigadier-General Anthony C. MacAuliffe, his Deputy Commander General MacAuliffe standing in for General Taylor, withstood the fierce German counter-attack in the Bastogne sector until 26th December 1944, when the divisional commander broke through the German lines to rejoin his garrison at Bastogne for the final battles.

the snow-covered slopes littered with dead troops and smashed tanks, and the half-frozen battle-exhausted troops and named the campaign the 'Alamo of Europe'. The troops of the besieged garrison had, however, already given themselves a title - less glamorous but alliteratively apt: 'Battered Bastards of the Bastogne Bastion'.

Major-General Taylor (plate 33) arrived with the Fourth Armoured to take command of his beloved 'battered bastards' and, working with combat teams of newly-arrived units, the Screaming Eagles swept through Foy and Noville and other small towns to the north of Bastogne. The 969th Field Artillery - the crack all-Negro 155mm 'Long Tom' outfit - hurled its huge missiles ahead of the advanced troops. Captured Germans (plate 34) milled in the prisoner-of-war cages. Von Rundsted's offensive had turned to defeat, largely through the epic courage of one American division - the 101st Airborne. (See plate 35.)

It should be remembered, however, that the important road centre of Bastogne could not have been held by the 101st without the aircraft of the Airborne Troop Carrier Command that delivered over 800,000 pounds of supplies to the division during the critical period between 22nd and 27th December 1944.

On 19th January 1945 the 101st was relieved from the Ardennes front and moved to a reassembly area. The 1st Battalion of the 504th Parachute Infantry Regiment received the Presidential Citation Streamer from General Gavin for the part it played in stopping von Rundstedt's 1.SS-Panzer-Grenadier-Division at the battle of Cheneux, Belgium. (See plate 36.) And the Eagle division was alerted for yet another mission - this time on the Alsace-Lorraine front.

The 17th Airborne Division and the Ardennes fighting

Activated in the United States, the 17th Airborne Division, commanded by General William Miley, was committed to the Ardennes battles. At the time of the German winter offensive, this new division was rapidly moved from the United Kingdom to France. The 17th Airborne (which with the 101st and the 82nd Airborne formed the XVIII Airborne Corps) was stationed close to the river Meuse and held in position while its area of greatest usefulness was determined. It was supported by the US 11th Armoured Division and the US 87th Infantry Division, also newly arrived in France. On the 28th December 1944 - the day after the Germans had launched their main thrust towards Bastogne - Eisenhower released the three new divisions to General Bradley. While the Screaming Eagles were becoming the heroes of Bastogne and the 'All Americans' were stopping and turning von Rundstedt on the northern flank, the 'Talons' - the 17th Airborne - were fully engaged in clawing away at the western perimeter of the besieged Bastogne garrison.

The 101st in the Ruhr fighting

With the move to the Alsace-Lorraine area, the 101st settled into defensive positions in Haguenau on the Moder river during February 1945. The Moder ran through the centre of Haguenau and the enemy held the north-east bank. For 31 days the division maintained its positions along the river. But for intensive patrol activity by both sides and the occasional heavy shelling of the town, however, the days in the line were relatively quiet. At the end of its engagement, in the spring of 1945, the division was withdrawn to France.

Back once more at Mourmelon-le-Grand the division rested, trained and was brought up to strength. And at an unprecedented ceremony held at camp Mourmelon, General of the Army Eisenhower - in the presence of Lieutenant-General Brereton, Commanding General of the 1st Allied Airborne Army, Major-General Ridgeway and a very proud Major-General Maxwell Taylor - awarded to the division the Presidential Unit Citation for its gallant defence of Bastogne. After a congratulatory address, General Eisenhower attached the citation streamer to the guidon of the Screaming Eagles Division. It was a unique occasion in the history of the American Army as it was the first time that an entire division had been given the citation. Previously, it had been awarded only to units of regimental or smaller size. For most units in the division, the citation meant an oak-leaf cluster added to the ribbon earned in the Normandy campaign.

The airborne crossing of the Rhine

The airborne crossing of the Rhine, code-named Varsity, proved to be not only the biggest airborne undertaking of the war but also the most successful.

Field Marshal Montgomery planned his ground assault across the Rhine on a front of four divisions - two from the British 21st Army Group (the 51st Highland Division and the 15th Scottish Division, supported by the 1st Commando Brigade) and two from the attached US Ninth Army (the 30th and 79th Infantry Divisions). Supporting them would be an airborne attack to be carried out by the American 17th Airborne Division (plate 38) and the British 6th Airborne Division, both under the command of the American XVIII Airborne Corps. The 17th Airborne Division had been chosen in preference to the 13th Airborne, which was newly arrived in Europe. (See plate 39.)

The ground forces' crossing was to be made under cover of darkness, to be followed the next morning by the airborne attack. The two airborne divisions were to drop close to the front lines, but not so close that they would come within the zone of the Allied artillery fire. From their position, they were to destroy the enemy's artillery organisation and participate directly in the tactical battle.

Preceded by a violent artillery barrage from the US Ninth Army front, in which 2,000 guns of all types participated, the ground assault was launched during the night of 23rd/24th March 1945. The Allied airborne troops began their assault at 1000 hours on the 24th. A total of 1,572 planes (plate 37) and 1,326 gliders (plate 1) carried them to their dropping zones and 899 fighters escorted them on their flight. Cover over the target area was provided by 2,153 other fighters that also established a defensive screen eastwards.

The 13th Airborne Division in Europe

The German Rhine defences in the Saar region were considered by the Allies to be sufficiently strong to require airborne forces to ensure a successful river crossing. Two airborne divisions were available for this undertaking - the American 17th and 13th. It fell to the latter - the 'Unicorn' division - to take on the task. But so great was the confusion of the Germans following the collapse of the Saar front that the airborne assault was stood down.

Out of a total of 61 American Army divisions committed to the fighting in the European theatre of operations, the 13th Airborne was the only formation that was never engaged in a battle.

34. *German troops taken prisoner during the relief of Bastogne awaiting transport to take them to the PoW cages.*

35. *Major-General Maxwell D. Taylor was presented with the Distinguished Service Medal by General Jacob L. Devers, Commanding General, VI US Army Group. General Taylor received the award for the 'operations' of his division in the vicinity of Bastogne, Belgium and the defence of that city, his expert planning, outstanding initiative, organizing ability and tireless devotion to duty inspiring all under him to great heights and remarkable combat achievement'.*

36. *Three airborne generals take the salute at the award ceremony held in Belgium for the 1st Battalion, 504th Parachute Infantry Regiment. From left to right: Lieutenant-General Lewis H. Brereton, Major-General Gavin and Major-General Ridgeway. General Brereton was appointed Commanding General of the 1st Allied Airborne Army upon its activation in 1944. Previously, he had been Commanding General of the 3rd US Air Force in July 1944, the 10th US Air Force in March 1942 and the 9th US Air Force in October 1942.*

37, 38 and 39. *Troops of the 17th Airborne Division prepare for the Rhine crossing.*

35

37

39

The end of the war in Europe

With the crossing of the Rhine behind them, the rest of the action in Europe for the American airborne formations was fierce but grounded - the 13th, 17th, 82nd and 101st airborne divisions, with the Troop Carrier Command and XVIII Airborne Corps, all having their parts to play.

When VE-Day came, the 82nd Airborne - fighting alongside the British - was 50 miles across the river Elbe, in Ludwigslust. It was here that it met up with the Russians on the northern front. On its way it had liberated the concentration camp at Wobbelin and accepted the surrender of the 145,000 German troops of the 21 Army commanded by Generalleutnant von Tippelskirch.

In late April 1945, the 101st Airborne Division moved from the Ruhr and started a wild chase that took the Eaglemen through southern Germany and on into the Bavarian Alps and Austria. The division was responsible for the capture of important German political and military figures such as Robert Ley (plate 43), Julius Streicher, Xavier Schwarz, Luftwaffe Feldmarschall Albert Kesselring (plate 44) and SS General Berger.

With units of the 1st French Army, the 101st captured Berchtesgaden (plate 45), liberated Göring's priceless art 'collection', and occupied Hitler's summer Reich Chancellery, the Eagle's Nest and the homes and offices of many other top Nazis. Units of the division moved to assignments of occupation in several villages in the Austrian Alps, a few miles across the German border.

After two months of rest in Bavaria and the Austrian villages, the division was moved back to Auxerre in France on 1st August 1945. The intention was that it would return to the States in 1946 after a stiff training programme; and then, after furlough, it would be sent to the Pacific. But the war ended before that could take place.

The troops of the 17th Airborne Division were split up and absorbed by the 82nd and 101st, the 17th becoming a redeployment vehicle.

The 82nd Airborne, strengthened by the men of the 17th Airborne and under the command of the American 1st Airborne Army, was appointed the task of administrating and policing the American sector of Berlin.

The 13th Airborne Division and the XVIII Airborne Corps were on their way to the Pacific when the atom bomb was dropped and the Japanese surrendered. Thereafter the XVIII Airborne Corps and the 1st Allied Airborne Army were both dispersed. The 101st and the 13th were absorbed into the 82nd Airborne Division.

40. *American troops of the 1st Allied Airborne Army come under enemy fire on the east bank of the Rhine.*
41. *An American jeep tows a light anti-tank gun out of a glider after landing east of the Rhine.*
42. *With bayonet fixed ready for close combat, a paratrooper approaches a house partly hidden by a parachute hanging from a tree.*
43. *Robert Ley, the leader of the German Labour Front, captured by troops of the 502nd Parachute Infantry Regiment.*
44. *Kesselring, with Maxwell Taylor, at the time of his capture on 9th May 1945.*
45. *General Bradley and officers of the 101st stand among the wreckage that was once Berchtesgaden.*
46. *Major-General C. R. Huebner and Major-General Taylor arriving in New York from Europe, 3rd June 1945.*

23

Uniforms

47. *The M1C (parachutist's) steel helmet.*

The uniforms, special clothing and equipment issued to and used by all members of the American airborne forces can be divided into two basic groups:

1. The special paratroop clothing and equipment that was designed for and issued to all members of the American airborne forces for training and for combat.

2. The uniforms with head-dress that were standard US Army issue to the infantry and which were also worn by or were available to the personnel of the airborne forces.

The formation of the first American airborne division, the 82nd, was brought about by converting the 82nd Infantry Division to an airborne role. Initially, therefore, all airborne personnel had the standard army clothing and equipment that was issued to the infantry. And the personnel of airborne formations raised subsequently during the war years continued to receive infantry clothing on activation or enlistment.

American Army dress regulations for all forms of issue clothing and equipment applied to the airborne forces; two factors, however, influenced the use of non-specialised airborne clothing:

1. The clothing used in the battle zone was governed by the type of combat role the airborne troops fulfilled.

2. The wearing by airborne troops of certain items of regulation clothing to the exclusion of alternative forms of dress.

Although both infantry and paratroops fought as ground forces, their differing modes of transport to the battle zones and the ways in which they fought had a direct bearing on what they wore. The regular infantry, which normally fought in the van of the army with the enemy at its front, was supplied by its own echelon troops. Additional clothing could be quickly supplied by ordinary or cross-country vehicles.

In contrast, in their normal airborne role paratroop forces were dropped behind the enemy lines with only the weapons and equipment they immediately required and the clothing they stood up in. Further essential supplies of ammunition, weapons, food and medical items took precedence over all else in subsequent air drops to the fighting airborne troops. Additional clothing could be flown in, but circumstances seldom if ever warranted it. The clothing used by these troops was therefore restricted to only the basic items essential to their combat role, and it had to be functional. It had to be capable of rough and prolonged wear. It needed to be at least showerproof, if not waterproof, and it had to be suited to prevailing climatic conditions. Furthermore, it had to fulfil certain requirements with regard to camouflage and concealment and to have adequate pockets to allow the wearer to carry additional ammunition, first aid and personal items.

1. AIRBORNE COMBAT CLOTHING

The four items that could be said to make up the distinctive combat clothing worn by the mass of American airborne troops operating in Europe were:

1. the M1C (parachutist's) steel helmet;
2. the airborne combat jacket;
3. the airborne combat trousers;
4. the airborne jump boots.

The M1C (Parachutist's) Steel Helmet

The M1C steel helmet was an issue item authorised for wear by all airborne personnel. Similar in appearance to the normal

48. *A paratroop officer leads his men in a demonstration jump-off.*

pattern M1 steel helmet, it differed slightly in the modified liner-strap system and had the noticeable addition of a chin cup. Like the M1 helmet, it consisted of two components: a steel shell and a liner. The liner, fashioned from hard, resilient fibre material, was fitted with web strap cushioning and was moulded to match the shape of the outer steel shell. (See plate 47.)

The two halves of the regular, adjustable helmet strap were anchored respectively to the left and right side of the rim of the helmet shell. The helmet was kept in position over the fibre liner by having the helmet chin-strap press-stud fastened to two short lengths of webbing strap that in turn were fitted to the left and right side of the liner. Under normal conditions, this was sufficient to hold both helmet components firmly together. (See plates 31, 52.)

However, paratroops were provided with two additional liner neck straps and a chin cup. (See plate 17.) These extra forked straps, positioned on either side of the liner, each ended in a small metal buckle. (See plate 2.) Attached to the two buckles were the strap ends of the moulded leather chin cup. (See plates 48, 49.) The chin cup straps were adjustable to hold the liner firmly in position on the wearer's head. With the steel shell securely fastened to the liner by the regular adjustable chin-strap as already described, this whole arrangement prevented the separation of the two components during parachute jumping.

When the steel helmet was worn by airborne personnel fighting a prolonged ground action, it could be easily and quickly converted to the normal infantry type. (See plate 8.) The chin cup could be unbuckled from the neck straps and the two sets of neck straps could be tucked in between the liner and helmet shell or up inside the liner cushioning straps. The regular helmet chin-strap was sufficient to keep the helmet on the wearer's head.

Helmet markings consisted, in the main, of painted rank insignia. (See plate 49.) Occasionally, interdivisional unit insignia would be painted on the sides of the helmet (see plate 33); and medical personnel were distinguished by painted Red Cross emblems. (See plate 51.)

Helmet netting in dark olive-drab was used on the steel helmets, sometimes with the addition of scrim. (See plate 18.) The netting provided the means of attaching the individual wound-dressing in a readily available place. (See plates 16, 50.)

The Airborne Combat Jacket
This issue garment was peculiar to American airborne forces. (See plate 52.) Its most distinctive feature was the shape and positioning of its four large patch pockets and pocket flaps. All the pockets were expandable and each had a straight-edged sloping flap secured by a pair of large smooth-surfaced press-stud fasteners. The two breast pockets, with inverted pleats, were positioned at an angle across the front of the chest. (See plate 17.) When correctly worn - that is, closed at the neck (plate 23) - the jacket was fastened by a concealed fly-fronted full-length heavy-duty metal zip. The collar was secured across the neck by two press-stud fasteners, and the sleeve cuffs were also fastened by press-studs.

Great care and attention went into the design of the special combined combat and jump jacket (and trousers) used by the airborne troops. Unlike the British Denison smock with its 'tail piece' and the German Fallschirmjäger smock with its 'legs', the American garment was more truly a combat jacket than a jump smock.

49 and 50. *The MIC steel helmet worn with netting cover (49) and with scrim attached to the netting (50).*

51. *American Red Cross marking worn painted on the parachute helmet.*

The Airborne Combat Trousers

The airborne combat trousers together with the combat jacket made up the official issue uniform worn by all American airborne personnel, regardless of rank, for training and combat. Matching the jacket in colour and quality of material, the trousers had normal side and hip pockets. An additional feature, however, were large distinctive thigh pockets - one to each leg. These expandable pockets had inverted pleats with press-stud fastened pocket flaps. (See plates 52, 53.)

It was these pockets that gave rise to the grim compliment afforded the American airborne troops by German prisoners: "Butchers in baggy pants." (See plate 53, 57.)

Strong webbing tapes were sewn into the inside-leg seams to allow the wearer to tie down and secure to his legs additional items of equipment, or weapons such as machetes, which had to be carried on air drops. (See plates 3, 54, 55, 59.) The ends of the trouser legs were usually worn tucked into the tops of the jump boots. (See plate 57.)

The Airborne Jump Boots

The high lace-up leather combat boots introduced in 1943 for wear by all army personnel, and intended to replace the high shoes and canvas leggins (plate 8), were very similar in appearance to the American airborne jump boots. They therefore tended to devalue the paratroopers jump boots as a distinctive item of apparel which, until then, had been proudly worn by airborne personnel as a token of identification. The front-lace-up high leather jump boots had been instantly recognisable as something that, along with the airborne unit or divisional insignia, set the paratrooper apart from the rest of the army. (See plates 3, 48, 54, 55, 57.)

2. INFANTRY CLOTHING FOR AIRBORNE PERSONNEL

The Service Uniform

The service uniform, for ordinary wear in the performance of duty, was of two kinds - woollen and cotton. Guided by the prevailing climatic conditions, the commanding officer would prescribe which should be worn by the enlisted men. Officers, however, could wear either at their own discretion.

The Winter and Summer Service Uniform Coats

The winter service coat was of dark olive-drab wool, and it was worn by all airborne personnel. All insignia and emblems had to be worn on the winter service coat.

The summer service coat was of khaki cotton, and with the matching quality trousers it formed the summer service uniform.

Displayed on both cuffs of officers' service coats - summer and winter - was a ½-inch-wide band of olive-drab braid. (See plate 46).

Regulations required that all coats - including the service coat - should be completely buttoned in all circumstances of wear.

The Service Uniform Trousers

These were of two types: the olive-drab (dark shade) trousers prescribed to be worn by airborne officers in the field (at times other than when the airborne combat trousers were worn) and by all other airborne personnel at all times other than in combat (olive-drab (dark shade) being the colour of the matching service coat); and the drab (light shade) trousers - or officers' 'pinks' - which were optional and could be worn when not in the field with any service coat, wool field jacket or shirt.

Personnel authorised to wear breeches were permitted to wear trousers when on duties other than those for which breeches were essential.

The Issue Waistbelt
A waistbelt was issued specifically for wear with the service trousers when the service shirt was worn without the coat. But it could be worn at other times. Of olive-drab web, it was 1¼ inches in width and it had a tongueless strap buckle. (See plate 31.)

The Service Shirt
Two types of service shirt were issued for wear throughout the US Army - the olive-drab and the khaki, manufactured from either woollen or cotton material. The woollen shirt was of worsted or gaberdine flannel (plate 43), and the other one was manufactured from olive-drab or khaki cotton broadcloth or cotton poplin. Either shirt was permitted to be worn when the service coat was worn.

Commanding officers could authorise the wearing of the olive-drab or the khaki service shirt without the service coat, in which case metal or embroidered insignia of grade and collar insignia were worn on the shirt in the prescribed manner. (See plates 25, 26, 31.) The wearing of an elasticated or any other form of armband grip was not permitted when the shirt was worn without the coat.

The Issue Necktie
The army issue necktie for wear by officers, warrant officers and enlisted men was of unpatterned cotton mohair, with neither stripe nor figure. Prior to February 1942 American troops were issued with both a khaki and a black necktie. The black necktie was to be worn with the service coat or when the olive-drab shirt was worn without the coat. However, the first American airborne troops were raised in August 1942 - six months after the black tie had been withdrawn from issue - and it is unlikely that they used it. The khaki necktie, which continued in use after February 1942, was originally to be worn only when the khaki shirt was worn without the service coat. After 1942, it was worn with all types of shirt, with and without the service coat. (See plate 26.) In the field, or under simulated field conditions, neckties were not permitted. (See plate 9).

When the shirt was worn without the coat, the necktie had to be tucked into the shirt between the first and second button. (See plate 25.)

The Wool Field Jacket, Model 1944.
This garment, first introduced in 1944 to replace the woollen service coat, immediately became a favourite item of apparel with the airborne forces because - unlike the service coat - it could be worn with the paratroopers jump boots. Apart from some senior airborne officers, almost all the airborne forces in Europe wore it to the total exclusion of the service coat. (See plates 25, 44, 46.)

With the exception of the officers' olive-drab cuff-braiding, all insignia and emblems as worn on the service coat were also required to be worn on the wool field jacket. (See plates 35, 44, 45, 46.)

Sweaters
The army issue high-necked sweater was a long-sleeved garment - machine knitted from dark olive-drab wool - that could be

52. Above: *Father and son, paratroopers from the 506th Parachute Infantry Regiment at Fort Benning, display an assortment of fighting weapons.*

53. Left: *The group-commander gets ready to lead his men in the jump-off as their plane approaches the dropping zone.*

worn buttoned up at the neck. In common with other regulation wool sweaters, it could be worn under the service coat or field jacket provided that it was not visible. It proved to be an especially convenient item of apparel for airborne troops operating in cold-weather conditions since they were unable to wear heavy overcoats.

The M1943 Field Jacket
Similar in general appearance to the airborne combat jacket, the four-pocket olive-drab Model 1943 field jacket was sometimes worn by airborne personnel. (See plates 27, 29, 36, 38, 39, 56.)

Army Overcoats
There were two kinds of overcoat: the long overcoat as an issue garment for wear by all ranks and the short overcoat for use by warrant officers, officers and generals only. Both styles were manufactured from olive-drab cloth - beaver, doeskin, kersey or melton. The buttons were of vegetable ivory or horn, conforming in colour to the material of the coat.

The Long Overcoat
This could be worn on duty only on the instruction of the commanding officer. Men off duty could wear it at will in cold or inclement weather. And officers were permitted to wear it on or off duty at their own discretion. The infantry occasionally wore it in combat during cold weather, but the paratroops were not equipped with it for combat air drops. It was a cumbersome garment in action and consequently, even in severe weather, it was seldom worn by airborne troops generally.

The Short Overcoat
This, again, was worn under instruction from the commanding officer - and when so authorised only one style of overcoat (Long or Short) was worn by all officers and warrant officers in a formation. The short overcoat was optional for the individual officer or warrant officer, but it was most favoured by senior officers and army generals. It had a matching cloth belt that did not necessarily have to be worn with it. The short overcoat was worn mainly by airborne officers and base personnel not actively involved in combat.

General officers - including airborne general officers - wore bands of black braid around the cuffs of their overcoats, both long and short. The lower band was 1¼ inches wide, and the narrow upper band was ½ inch wide. (See plate 36).

Military-style Raincoats and Waterproof Trench Coats
Raincoats and trench coats were occasionally worn by airborne officers in conditions that warranted their use (See plate 36). But the officers had to purchase them privately. Stipulations were that they had to be of a commercial pattern, with shoulder loops, and as near as possible to olive-drab in colour. They also had to be waterproof, hard-wearing and resistant to tearing; and they had to reach to at least below the knees.

All enlisted men were issued with a standard pattern military raincoat, but it was seldom if ever used by airborne personnel within a combat zone.

The Service Cap
This form of head-dress was authorised for wear by all officers and warrant officers when not in formation with troops and also by enlisted men assigned to corps area service commands or to

54. Top: *An early-morning shave.*

55. *A paratrooper fully kitted out with his equipment, harness, weapons and ammunition.*

56. **Far right:** *A soldier from the 17th Airborne Division wearing the Model 1943 field jacket.*

the War Department. In practice, however, it was seldom worn by the majority of airborne troops. Instead they preferred to wear their garrison caps, which displayed their distinctive airborne patches. The service cap was used, however, by senior airborne officers and airborne generals.

The Garrison Cap
There were two types of garrison cap (formerly known as the field or overseas cap) - one for summer wear and one for winter wear. The prescribed material was khaki cotton cloth or khaki tropical worsted material for the summer and dark olive-drab wool for the winter. All Army personnel were authorised to wear the cap. For general officers it was piped with cord-edged braid of gold bullion, rayon or metallised cellophane of gold colour. Other officers had cord-edged braid of gold bullion, rayon or metallised cellophane intermixed with black silk. Cap piping for warrant officers was as for officers but in silver with black silk intermixed. For airborne enlisted men the cap was piped with light blue cord.

In defiance of US Army Dress Regulations, the garrison cap was given a very individualistic look by the majority of American airborne troops in the European Theatre of operations - with the crown crushed down and shaped to form peaks at the front and rear of the cap. (See plate 43.)

Cap Insignia
Rank insignia for airborne officers, in conformity with normal US Army practice, was displayed on the left side and towards the front of the garrison cap. (See plate 35.) Enlisted men displayed the paratroop, glider or combined para-glider circular cloth cap-badge (patch) on the left side of the cap towards the front. (See plate 43). When an officer was qualified to wear one of the three airborne patches, the emblem was displayed on the right side of the garrison cap as opposed to his insignia of rank on the left side. (See plates 43, 45.)

Shoes
Apart from the habitual wearing of the parachute jump boots by airborne troops, almost as a mark of pride, plain brown leather shoes were worn with plain tan or brown socks for walking out, office duty, social functions and the like. (See plate 44.)

Rubber Overshoes
The commanding officer would prescribe the wearing of overshoes when conditions warranted their use. They were mainly worn by airborne base personnel at camps where the ground was wet and muddy.

Canvas Leggins
Standard issue army canvas leggins were initially used by all officers and enlisted men of the infantry divisions that were later converted to an airborne role. The leggins were part of the normal issue infantry equipment. However, the special lace-up airborne jump boots - which were high and of leather - made the wearing of canvas leggins unneccesary. Nevertheless, although the occasions were rare, airborne personnel sometimes used them (See plate 7).

Gloves
Normal issue army gloves were worn by airborne personnel when conditions required them. The service gloves were of

leather or wool-knit, or a combination of leather and olive-drab cloth. Unlike their German counterparts, American paratroopers had no special issue of gloves as part of their combat clothing. (See Plate 36.)

Army Identification Tags

Identification tags were prescribed to be worn by all members of the American armed forces, including airborne personnel, at all times. These metal tags were worn suspended around the neck by a thin metal chain 40 inches in length. Each tag was embossed with the owner's name, army number, religion, information regarding inoculations and blood type. The tags were regarded as part of the military uniform and had to be worn constantly by the owner.

Notes on American airborne badges and shoulder sleeve insignia

The terms 'shoulder patches' and 'divisional insignia' were in common usage during the First World War, but during the Second World War 'shoulder sleeve insignia' became the official designation and remained in use thereafter. (See colour reference section 2.)

The Stars and Stripes arm flag: A representation of the national flag of the United States was worn either on an armband or sewn to the sleeve as an identification badge for the American forces that landed in North Africa, Normandy and on the Rhine. (See plate 50.)

82nd Airborne Division: The original shoulder sleeve insignia for the First World War infantry division was approved on 21st October 1918. It consisted of a red square containing a blue disc bearing the white letters 'AA' in monogram form. The same 'All American' insignia was reintroduced when the 82nd Infantry Division was reactivated, and on 31st August 1942 permission was granted for the addition of the word 'Airborne' in white on a blue ground on an arched tab over the shoulder sleeve insignia. (See plate 27.)

101st Airborne Division: The original shoulder sleeve insignia for the 101st Infantry Division was approved on 23rd May 1923. It was the head, in profile, of a screaming eagle, in white, with a golden beak set on a black 'eared' shield. After the division had been reactivated, during the Second World War, the black tab with gold-lettered 'Airborne' was added on 28th August 1942. (See plates 30, 35, 45.) The original 101st had been raised in Wisconsin, which had an American Civil War military tradition upon which the design of shoulder sleeve insignia was based. The black shield recalls the 'Iron Brigade' of which Company C, The Eau Claire Eagles, from the 8th Wisconsin Regiment possessed the famous war eagle 'Old Abe'. According to legend a Chippewa Indian, Chief Sky, captured an eaglet on the Flambeau river, Wisconsin, in 1861 and sold the bird for a bushel of corn. A subsequent purchaser, having paid five dollars for it, gave the eagle to Company C of the 8th Wisconsin Regiment. The story goes that the eagle, tethered to a shield and carried by a sergeant between the national Colour and the regimental Colour, was carried into battle as a mascot. 'Old Abe' would fly to the end of his tether and screech out his defiance at the enemy, giving the company new vigour and hope. The eagle went through thirty-six battles and was wounded first in the assault on Vicksbury and then in the Battle of Corinth, during which engagement the

57, 58 and 59. The interiors of American transport aircraft.

Confederate General Sterling Price is said to have offered a reward for the bird's capture or death.

The 101st Airborne Division also adopted an eagle as its mascot when at Fort Bragg in North Carolina, and they named it 'Young Abe'. Unfortunately, it died at Fort Bragg while the division was undergoing training in Tennessee.

17th Airborne Division: This division's shoulder sleeve insignia consisted of an eagle's talon in gold - hence its nickname of the 'Talon' division - set on a circular black background above which was displayed the title 'Airborne', also in gold-yellow on black.

13th Airborne Division: The 'Unicorn' division - as its nickname implies - had a yellow winged unicorn set in a blue shield above which was the title 'Airborne'.

XVIII US Airborne Corps: The corps' shoulder sleeve insignia consisted of a dragon's head with a barbed tongue in blue, set on a square white background within a blue border. Again, the 'Airborne' tab appeared above the insignia, this time in blue and white.

The Para-Glider Garrison Cap Patch: In an effort to abolish the distinction that had built up between glidermen and paratroopers, and to make 'airborne' the criterion, a new form of airborne cap insignia was introduced in the spring of 1943 combining the parachute and glider emblems. It was worn on the garrison cap by all ranks - on the right-hand side by officers and on the left-hand side by all other personnel. (See plates 43, 45.)

60. *The CG-4A gliders, towed by the C-47 cargo plane, was capable of carrying fifteen soldiers or a load consisting of jeeps or motor cycles.*

The Parachutist's Qualification Badge: This silver metal badge was authorised for personnel who had passed proficiency, educational and fitness tests for qualified parachutists. It was also awarded for a combat parachute jump without prior training. The badge was 1½ inches in length and represented an open parachute flanked on either side by sculptured wings curving up and inwards, their tips joining the edge of the parachute canopy. The badge was approved on 10th March 1941 and was worn over the left breast pocket. (See plates 31, 35.)

Airborne Command: This shoulder sleeve insignia consisted of a red Norman shield displaying a glider above an open parachute in white. The 'Airborne' tab was black with yellow lettering.

First Allied Airborne Army: Worn by both American and British personnel, this insignia consisted of a grey-green shield of which the upper portion was black with the words 'Allied Airborne' in yellow. In the centre of the shield was a large figure '1' in white flanked by yellow wings and standing on a bright red base. On this base were two short Roman swords, crossed, in white.

The Second Airborne Infantry Brigade: This brigade was made up of the 507th and 508th Parachute Infantry Regiments, which fought alongside the 82nd Airborne Division in Normandy. The brigade shoulder sleeve insignia consisted of an upright rectangular patch with rounded ends divided in half vertically by a line of interlocking joints. The right side had a white sword on a blue ground, and the left side had a blue sword on a white ground. The 'Airborne' tab was black with yellow letters.